Appreciating Art

Debbie and Darrel Trulson

Ad Maiorem

Dei Gloriam

• A PUBLICATION OF •

Christian Liberty Press

502 West Euclid Avenue, Arlington Heights, Illinois 60004

Table of Contents

Introduction

Art is a God-given vehicle whereby mankind can reflect the glory of the Creator by expressing some aspect of beauty, diversity or creativity. When people talk about "art", they frequently have different ideas from the next person. One may think of art in terms of a statue or a fine painting, while another may think of a child's crayon marks on the wall or their own arrangement of fresh flowers in a vase that catches the light just so. None of these images are any more deserving of artistic merit than another. Indeed, each idea of beauty and creativity is unique to the individual. Some may express their artistry through the mediums of paint or pen, while others may speak through wood or clay. The possible outlets for exhibiting our God-given talents are too numerous to detail here; yet, they are at your fingertips, available to be used as an extension of yourself.

Art is truly a creative, expressive and enriching part of our everyday lives. As you use the information contained within these pages, you must picture yourself as an observer rather than an instructor. Your child is giving you the opportunity to experience a bit of his world through his unleashing of creative skills. After initially providing the materials and location, exchange ideas together. Your main objective should be to create a time of sharing, fun and discovery rather than a "perfect" specimen of a craft.

Many young children and even some adults have had the joy of artistic endeavors forever robbed from them through the rigid, narrow-minded ideas of a teacher or other person who views himself as holding the answers to "the right way to do things". In your teaching, it is imperative that you leave behind old baggage you may carry about art and begin with a fresh outlook.

It is the authors' desire that all who use this book will take time to reflect on that which is art around them. One does not need to own a Renoir or Degas to appreciate artistic beauty and presence. To make the teaching of creativity a whole-life experience, one must go beyond pre-designed curricula and begin to incorporate this philosophy into their daily life.

For instance, add a centerpiece to your dinner table tonight which you or your child have created. Appreciate the beauty of handmade baskets or quilts. Savor the kitchen artistry of home-baked bread or a fragrant marinara sauce. Contemplate the differences of expression in a Rembrandt, Chagall or Michelangelo. Once all of your senses have awakened to the beauty which surrounds you, it is then, you will be able to share with your child an education that far exceeds any workbook, or cut and paste session. Stretching one's mind to see past the ordinary is an important part of any person's education. Art appreciation is only the beginning. The canvas awaits; now you must pick up the brush.

BEFORE YOU BEGIN

As you work, keep in mind that although the crafts are arranged under certain sections, they could very easily fit elsewhere. If it suits your purpose to rearrange them, then by all means do so.

We also recommend that you begin saving scraps of fabric, ribbon, broken strings of beads, etc., in a box set aside expressly for your child's artistic creations. Our intent is not to send you scurrying to every craft and art supply store looking for obscure items, but instead, to encourage you and your child to be resourceful by using what is easily accessible.

You will note, that at the end of each lesson there is an intensity level rating. This star system is based on a 1-4 scale, with 1 being less difficult or time consuming, progressing to 4 which should have a greater time or material allotment. This should help you in planning your schedule and level of patience on a given day.

*The drawing on the Title page was created by our son Daniel when he was eight years old.

Section I Introduction

Before beginning this section containing "Art in the Kitchen", take time to examine your ideas and attitudes surrounding the kitchen. Does your child see you experiencing the kitchen with a creative and enthusiastic outlook? Is your kitchen an organized and pleasant place in which to congregate and work? If you were able to answer those questions in the affirmative, then your child is probably already skilled in some basic kitchen tasks. If you had a negative response to those questions, here is your opportunity to approach your kitchen with a fresh outlook. Since many of a child's memories are centered around this one room, it is hard to ignore its importance. Let this be your opportunity to do some memory building with your child!

"When one has tasted watermelons, one knows what angels eat."
--Mark Twain

"The Queen of Hearts, she made some tarts, all on a summers day. The Knave of Hearts, he stole those tarts, and gave them quite away!"
--Lewis Carroll

Old Johnny Appleseed

A long time ago, when the early settlers of Ohio still lived in little log cabins in the midst of a lonely wilderness, there wandered from farm to farm an interesting, but lovable old man. Johnny Appleseed he was called, though his real name was John Chapman. He brought the little country girls ribbons and small cheery pieces of calico, and all the children loved him. Years before, Johnny Appleseed had given away to a poor woman with a large and needy family, his home at Pittsburgh Landing. He then tied two Indian canoes together and packed them to the rim with deer-skin bags full of apple seeds. Then he drifted off with the current down the Ohio River, having only one wish in his heart, to make people happier and more at home in the wilderness by planting apple trees.

Now farms were far apart in those days, with long, lonely stretches between billowy, tree-less prairies, or shadowy old forests, where bears, deer, wolves, and Indians wandered about. Men, women and children toiled hard to raise the simplest food; and for fruit, they had only berries and sour wild plums or crabs. They had no friendly apple trees to comfort them. Naturally, they longed for an evening with juicy, round, red apples, munched by all the family about the open fire. Often the hearts of those pioneers were heavy with homesick longing, as they thought of the low rambling farmhouses left far away in the east, so cozy and peaceful beneath the pink and white glory of blossoming apple trees.

Old Johnny knew how they felt. Old Johnny knew what they wanted. The greatest adventure in life to him was to wander off in the wilderness and plant his precious seeds. Every year he gathered the seeds that were thrown away from the cider-presses in Western Pennsylvania. Then he tramped back with his load all the way to Ohio.

Along the road he trudged, merrily whistling a tune, but dressed in nothing whatever except a coffee sack with holes for his arms and head. As a hat, he wore an old tin pan wherein he had cooked his mush, or a homemade pasteboard contraption, with a peak, like a roof, extending far out in front to protect his eyes from the sun. Usually he was barefooted. Only when snow lay deep on the ground was he sometimes to be seen with a cast-off boot on one foot and a moccasin on the other. Aye, he was strange, was Old Johnny; yet no one ever laughed at him. They loved him far too dearly.

Sometimes the pioneers paid Johnny small sums for his seeds or the tiny snips of trees which he grew in his different nurseries, but he never thought of spending his money on buying clothes for himself. No, he gave it away to some unfortunate family, and every fall he gathered together the poor, old, worn-out horses turned adrift by the settlers, buying food for them until Spring, when he led them away to pasture.

Often people asked Johnny if he was not afraid to wander about barefooted. In that land, other men wrapped up their legs in bandages of dried grass. They thought even buckskin leggings not tough enough to protect them from the sting of snakes which abounded in the tall, strong, prairie grass. But Johnny only replied that he was afraid of nothing. He loved every creature that God had made and so he tramped through the forest, fearless, safe and free. Mother bears let him play with their cubs and even the Indians loved him. He would not carry a gun and yet they never harmed him. Too many times had he done them some little kindness.

In the war of 1812, when the Indians broke out savagely against the lone settlers along the frontiers of the West, they still let Johnny go free, safe and unmolested through the narrow trails of the woods. And, though he did not fight, he often wandered for days, sleepless and taking no food, but giving alarm of attacks intended by the Indians, and warning the pioneers to flee to the nearest blockhouse.

One brilliant moonlight night he thrilled the heart of a farmer by thundering forth his message as though he had been a prophet out of the Bible that he loved:

"The spirit of the Lord is upon me and He hath anointed me to sound an alarm in the forest; for behold the tribes of the heathen are round about your doors!"

With all his heart Johnny believed that God had sent him forth to preach the gospel of love and to plant his apple seeds. When he came to a cabin at nightfall and the family sat about the fire, he would stretch himself out on the floor and ask the little group if they wished to hear "some news right fresh from heaven." Then he would take out his Bible and read the words of Jesus, his voice now strong and loud as the roar of the wind and waves, and now sinking soft and low and soothing as summer breezes.

Once a wandering preacher, talking under the treetops and scolding his listeners roundly, cried aloud with importance: "Where now is a man who, like the early Christians, is traveling to heaven barefoot and clothed in coarsest raiment?"

Suddenly Johnny rose from the log on which he sat.

"Here is your early Christian," he pointed to his coffee sack, and the preacher hung his head. He himself was not ready to lead such a simple life of quiet, unselfish deeds, and so he dismissed his hearers and quickly slunk away.

"Slowly many people came pressing into the wilderness. Towns and churches appeared and stage coaches broke, with the blare of their horns, the ancient, peaceful stillness of prairies and age-old forests. So in 1858 Johnny said farewell to his friends and turned his face farther westward, to spend his last nine years still in advance of settlement, far on the western frontiers, even pressing as far as Casey, Illinois. And when, after forty years, his long unselfish labors came to an end, how richly they had borne fruit! One hundred thousand square miles in Ohio and Indiana bore witness to the labors of one stout-hearted old hero, who had no thought for himself, but planted his little brown seeds in order that men and women, youths and maids and children, whom he had never seen, should some day eat rosy apples around their glowing hearths, and wander in the Springtime beneath the fragrant branches of blossoming apple trees.

Lesson 1
Making Butter

PURPOSE:
This lesson will demonstrate how butter is made and the joy one can experience in being resourceful.

MATERIALS NEEDED:
* Whipping cream or heavy cream (not ultra-pasteurized)
* Salt
* Wide mouth quart jar with a tight fitting lid
* Colander

INSTRUCTIONS:
Allow the cream to sit at room temperature for a few hours. Fill your jar about half full with cream and screw the lid on tightly. Holding the jar by both ends, shake it vigorously for about 15 or 20 minutes. Extra shakers (i.e. family members or friends) could be a big help here! After a while the cream will begin to separate and the butter will come. When you are finished, the butter in the jar should be about the mass of a baseball.

Pour off the liquid (this is the buttermilk which you can save--our children loved drinking it), and rinse the butter curd in a colander under cold water to remove any milk. You should rinse until the water runs clear. After this, you may add a pinch or two of salt for flavor. Mold your butter or pack it in a small cup and refrigerate. You now have homemade butter to enjoy, and everyone gave their arms a workout in the process.

FINAL THOUGHTS:
In past generations, the job of churning butter fell to the children. As they worked, they would often invent rhymes to make the process more enjoyable. The rhyme which follows is actually a very old churning rhyme which children long ago chanted. Teach it to your child as they shake the butter.

> *Come butter come.*
> *Come butter come.*
> *Peter standing at the gate,*
> *waiting for a butter cake.*
> *Come butter come.*

INTENSITY LEVEL: * * (Two Stars)

Lesson 2
Imaginative Drawing Mystery Fruit

PURPOSE:
This lesson introduces a drawing concept which will be repeated at various times in following lessons. Imaginative drawing is a superior alternative to coloring sheets and books, because this type of drawing will encourage your student to be more creative and self-expressive.

MATERIALS NEEDED:
* Art Pattern #6 (page 71)
* Drawing tools of your choice (colored pencils, pens, markers, crayons, etc.)

INSTRUCTIONS:
Before you begin the lesson, explain the concept to your child of using his own imagination to finish drawing a picture. If your child is acquainted with ordinary coloring sheets, this may be difficult for him to understand right away. In this lesson we are encouraging him to be the artist and the "idea person", not to simply color someone else's picture. Please do not tell your child that his drawing is wrong or too silly, just allow the freedom of artistic expression to govern his creativity.

One day, a child went walking through the woods near his home. He happened to see a tree which caught his attention. On it hung the most interesting fruit he had ever seen. It had a strange shape and was brightly colored. Not knowing if it was safe to eat, but being curious none-the-less, he picked one of the fruit from the tree and brought it home to show his parents. Together, they discovered that this fruit was a new variety of apple, even though it didn't look like an apple. Wondering what it tasted like, they cut it into pieces and found to their amazement that it was the most delicious fruit they had ever eaten.

Immediately, they left their home and went into the woods where the child had discovered the amazing tree. Though they searched as hard as they could, they were not able to find the tree which had produced this precious fruit. Somehow, the apple tree was gone.

When they returned home, they went into the kitchen and looked longingly at the place where they had eaten the delicious apple. Nothing was left on their plates except the stem and one small seed. Then the thought

occurred to them, "Why don't we plant that seed and see if we can grow our own apple tree." And that is just what they did.

As the years went by, the seed sprouted, developed into a strong sapling, and grew into a healthy tree, but it still didn't produce any fruit. By now the child, who first found the tree, was grown and married with children of his own. Whenever he would return to his home and visit his parents, he would take his children for a walk under the apple tree, and tell them his interesting story. As the children listened to their father speak, they would color pictures of this mysterious fruit which tasted so good. Someday they knew, this tree would have its own fruit and they would be able to enjoy it for themselves.

Using Art Pattern #6, ask your child to draw a picture of this amazing fruit on the tree. Your student can be the child in the story who found the tree. Now they have to draw a picture of it so everyone in the world will know what it looks like.

FINAL THOUGHTS:
It is important to reiterate that you should not interfere with the child's self expression in this project. You may help suggest ideas, of course, particularly if he is experiencing difficulty in getting started. However, let him draw and color his fruit any way he prefers.

INTENSITY LEVEL: * (One Star)

> Rather than creativity being squashed out it should be enhanced and developed because of being brought up in a Christian home, not in spite of it!
> --Edith Schaeffer, The Hidden Art of Homemaking

Lesson 3
Beans in a Bottle

PURPOSE:
This lesson provides your child with the opportunity to create an interesting layered effect which can be redesigned over and over.

MATERIALS NEEDED:
Choose from this list or add your own choice of bottle ingredients:
* Variety of beans (kidney, green pea, yellow pea, pinto, navy, garbanzo, lentil, etc.)
* Popcorn kernels (plain, colored or both)
* Bird seed
* Rice
* Large, clear, empty bottle (this can be a mayonnaise or ketchup jar or any other available jar with a lid)
* Pans or bowls to separate ingredients

INSTRUCTIONS:
Separate all the ingredients and allow your child to begin layering and experimenting. This does not have to be finished at once. If the jar is large, your child may wish to spend a couple of days designing his pattern. Once it is completed, the bottle may be sealed and displayed or rearranged to create another pattern.

You may want to remind your child that if he wants the ingredients to "layer" nicely, he will have to put the larger items (kidney beans and kernels) on the top and the smaller items (bird seed and rice) on the bottom. Otherwise, as the jar is "jiggled," the smaller items will begin sifting down to the bottom.

FINAL THOUGHTS:
Bottles are great mediums for displaying a wide range of items. We use old, blue Mason jars for showcasing potpourri and a button collection. These jars are rather plentiful at flea markets and antique stores, and they are still a good bargain. Think about your families various collections and perhaps you may come up with some interesting "stuff in a bottle" yourself!

INTENSITY LEVEL: * * * (Three Stars)

Lesson 4
Applesauce Parfaits

PURPOSE:
In this lesson, your child will create their own layered snack or dessert using two basic ingredients.

MATERIALS NEEDED:
* Applesauce
* Graham crackers (3 or 4 crackers for each serving)
* Zip-top or twist-tie plastic bag
* Two small bowls
* Clear glass or parfait-type glasses

INSTRUCTIONS:
Place the graham crackers in the plastic bag and seal tightly. Your child must now crunch and pound the bag to make fine crumbs of the graham crackers. Once the crumbs are made, pour them into a small bowl. Pour some applesauce into the other bowl and now begin layering. Your child can begin with either ingredient for the first layer and continue alternating until the desired level is reached. Once the creation is complete all that is left is to eat and enjoy!!!

FINAL THOUGHTS:
It is best to make this treat shortly before eating, as the crumbs tend to get soggy otherwise.

For a sugar-free parfait, use fruit-juice sweetened grahams and unsweetened applesauce. If that is not your need or interest, you can try cinnamon-sugar grahams and add a little cinnamon to the applesauce for a different flavor.

If you have children of various ages, they can all join in the making of this treat. Even our 2 1/2 year old loved pounding the crackers, and the eleven year old took great care in making precise layers.

INTENSITY LEVEL: * * (Two Stars)

Lesson 5
Snack on a String

PURPOSE:
In this lesson, your child will make and eat their own jewelry creation.

MATERIALS NEEDED:
*   Dental floss cut to desired necklace length
*   Large-eyed needle
*   A selection of various snacks (for example: any dry cereal with a center hole; raisins or other dried fruit; gum drops; beef jerky; popcorn)

INSTRUCTIONS:
Place the snacks in small cups or bowls and have your child begin threading his choices on the floss. He can make one for each member of the family or even a couple for himself. Once the "chain" is complete, tie the ends in a secure knot, and it is ready to be enjoyed.

FINAL THOUGHTS:
These "chains" can be worn around the neck and eaten on a hike or car trip, but they will work just as well around the house. Perhaps your child could eat his snack during a story or while playing a game. However you choose to use this activity, you may find yourself, like us, repeating the project again because it comes in so handy.

INTENSITY LEVEL: * * * (Three Stars)

Small cheer and great welcome makes a merry feast.
--William Shakespeare

Lesson 6
Elements of Shape

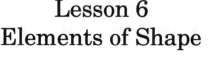

PURPOSE:
In this lesson, your child will learn about the five elements of shape. These shapes are the basic components to all drawing. The better we understand these shapes, the more clearly we can focus on our intended design.

MATERIALS NEEDED:
* Art Pattern #1, #2 and #3 (pages 59, 61 and 63)
* Extra white paper
* Colored pencils, crayons, or markers

INSTRUCTIONS:
Review Art Pattern #1 and explain the different shapes to your child. Using Art Pattern #2, have your child draw the different elements of shape where they are missing. In addition, you may also want to have him draw the elements of shape on a blank sheet of paper. It is important to have a good understanding of the different shapes before moving on to the next Art Pattern.

When your child has a good understanding of the five elements of shape, take Art Pattern #3 and have him draw the eagle in the stages illustrated. The drawing of this figure is simply a connection of the five basic shapes. Point out to your child each of the different shapes as he draws them. This exercise may also be repeated on a blank sheet of paper.

FINAL THOUGHTS:
Have your child look around the house to find the five elements of shape in the different things he sees. What elements are present in a spoon, picture, glass, car, or anything else he may come across? Discuss these shapes with your child, and point out how each of the shapes are connected and related to one another.

For further information on the elements of shape, you may want to read the book, Drawing with Children, written by Mona Brookes. Many of the ideas from this lesson come from there. The idea of the eagle came from Ed Emberley's Drawing Book of Faces. Ed Emberley has written several books on drawing and is highly recommended for children from ages 3 to 103.

We will be doing more work in drawing and use of the elements of shape in future lessons, so hold on to your "elements of shape" sheets for future reference.

INTENSITY LEVEL: * * (Two Stars)

Lesson 7
Puffed Cereal Balls

PURPOSE:

In this lesson, your child will make his own snack and at the same time, become more familiar with working in the kitchen.

MATERIALS NEEDED:
* 1/2 cup chunky peanut butter
* 1/3 cup honey
* 1/2 cup flaked coconut
* 2 cups puffed cereal (wheat, oat, rice)
* Mixing bowl
* Measuring cups
* Mixing spoon
* Medium size bowl

INSTRUCTIONS:

In the mixing bowl, stir together the peanut butter, honey and coconut. Mix well. Stir in 1/2 cup of the cereal. Place the leftover cereal in the medium bowl. Scoop out a heaping tablespoon of the peanut butter mixture and have your child roll it into a ball, and then, roll it in the cereal until it is coated. This makes a sweet and nutritious snack for an indoor or outdoor picnic!

FINAL THOUGHTS:

In the winter you can provide a respite from the "cold weather blues", if you ignore any messes and create an indoor picnic. Use this recipe and others like it, then choose a cozy spot, lay down a blanket, and dine "al fresco" -- well almost!

During the summer, our children eat lunch outside nearly every day. Even an ordinary lunch is more fun when you change the surroundings. They also pack food in their wagon and walk to the park where they can eat and play (or maybe it's the other way around)! Just keep in mind that the important thing is to enjoy food and celebrate the pleasure of even the simplest culinary delight.

INTENSITY LEVEL: * * (Two Stars)

Lesson 8
Bakers Clay Sculpting

PURPOSE:

In this lesson, your child will take a step beyond play dough by sculpting a permanent creation.

MATERIALS NEEDED:
* 4 cups flour
* 1 cup salt
* 1 1/2 cups cold water
* Lightly floured board or table
* Oven
* Cookie sheet
* Acrylic or tempra paints (optional)
* Shellac (optional)

INSTRUCTIONS:

Stir together flour, salt and water until everything is well blended. Turn the dough out onto a lightly floured board and knead vigorously for about five minutes, until a smooth, pliable dough is formed. Add some extra flour to the board, if necessary, to prevent sticking in the early stages of kneading. Dough should <u>not</u> be sticky.

Allow your child to design his sculpture. Once completed, bake at 350 degrees for 50-60 minutes or until solid and ivory/tan in color. Cool completely. Decorate or paint and spray with shellac. Do keep in mind, that the clay will dry out quickly and must be baked 5-6 hours after combining the ingredients.

FINAL THOUGHTS:

If you want to promote the theme of Johnny Appleseed, you could suggest that your child sculpt an apple, (maybe even one with a bite out of it). Of course, paint would be a good idea here in order to make it more realistic. If you want to help with the visualization of the object, you may wish to place a "model" apple in front of your child.

Bakers clay can also be used for making necklace beads. Simply roll pieces into balls or other small shapes, make a hole through them and bake. These are great to paint with wild designs for "fun jewelry".

INTENSITY LEVEL: * * * (Three Stars)

Section II Introduction

As you enter this section on "Art for Others", it would be advisable to look through the various projects and decide who among your friends and family would enjoy these handmade items. Your objectives are three-fold. First, you want the gift to be appreciated. If your child has put effort into his creation, it will be a real confidence boost to him to see his gift displayed and cherished. Secondly, you want to give your child a hands-on example of considering another person's needs and interests. For example, maybe Grandma would love the silhouette from Lesson 13; whereas Aunt Darla would enjoy the wire ornament in Lesson 11 for her Christmas tree. Encourage your child to see people's individual preferences as another fascinating aspect of human nature. Most of all, take this time to reinforce the joy of giving from the heart.

"You have been my friend," replied Charlotte. "That in itself is a tremendous thing. I wove my webs for you because I liked you. After all, what's a life, anyway? We're born, we live a little while, we die. A spider's life can't help being something of a mess, with all this trapping and eating flies. By helping you, perhaps I was trying to lift up my life a trifle. Heaven knows anyone's life can stand a little of that."
--E. B. White *Charlotte's Web*

The Tongue-Cut Sparrow

In a little house in a little old village in Japan, lived a little old man and his little old wife.

One cold morning when the old woman slid open the screens which form the sides of the Japanese houses, she saw on the doorstep a poor little sparrow. He was freezing and almost dead, but she took him up gently and fed him. Then she held him in the bright sunshine until the cold dew was dried from his wings. Afterward she let him go, so that he might fly home to his nest; but he stayed to thank her with his songs.

Each morning, when the pink on the mountain tops told that the sun was near, the sparrow perched on the roof of the house and sang out his joy.

The old man and woman thanked the sparrow for this, for they liked to be up early and at work. But near them lived a mean old woman who did not like birds, or music, or anyone who was happy. At last she became so angry that she caught the sparrow and cut his tongue. Then the poor little sparrow flew away to his home. But he never could sing again.

When the kind woman discovered what had happened to her little friend she was very sad. She said to her husband, "Let us go and find our poor little sparrow." So they started together, and asked of each bird by the wayside: "Do you know where the tongue-cut sparrow lives? Do you know where the tongue-cut sparrow went?"

In this way they followed until they came to a bridge. They did not know which way to turn, and at first could see no one to ask.

At last they saw a bat, hanging head downward, taking his day-time nap. "O, friend Bat, do you know where the tongue-cut sparrow went?" they asked.

"Yes. Over the bridge and up the mountain," said the bat. Then he blinked his sleepy eyes and was fast asleep again.

They went over the bridge and up the mountain, but again they found two roads and did not know which one to take. A little field mouse peeped through the leaves and grass, so they asked him, "Do you know where the tongue-cut sparrow went?"

"Yes. Down the mountain and through the woods," said the field mouse.

Down the mountain and through the woods they went, and at last came to the home of their little friend.

When he saw them coming the poor little sparrow was very happy indeed. He and his wife and children all came and bowed their heads down to the ground to show their respect. Then the sparrow rose and led the old man and the old woman into the house, while his wife and children hastened to bring them boiled rice, fish, and cress.

After they had feasted, the sparrow family wished to please them still more, so the children flew around the old man and woman and sang beautiful songs.

When the sun began to sink, the old man and woman started home, but before they left the sparrow brought out two baskets. "I would like to give you one of these," he said. "Which will you take?" One basket was large and looked very full, while the other one seemed very small and light. The old people thought they would not take the large basket, for that might have all the sparrow's treasure in it, so they said, "The way is long, so please let us take the smaller one."

They took it and walked home over the mountain and across the bridge, happy and contented.

When they reached their own home they decided to open the basket and see what the sparrow had given them. Within the basket they found many rolls of silk and piles of gold, enough to make them rich, so they were more grateful than ever to the sparrow.

The mean old woman who had cut the sparrow's tongue was peering through the screen when they opened the basket. She saw the rolls of silk and piles of gold, and planned how she might get some for herself.

The next morning she went to the kind woman and said, "I am so sorry that I cut the tongue of your sparrow. Please tell me the way to his home so that I may go to him and tell him I am sorry."

The kind old woman told her the way and she set out. She went across the bridge, over the mountain, and through the woods. At last she came to the home of the little sparrow.

He was not so glad to see this old woman, yet he was very kind to her and did everything to make her feel welcome. They made a feast for her, and when she started home the sparrow brought out two baskets as before. Of course the woman chose the large basket, for she thought that would have even more treasure than the other one.

It was very heavy, and caught on the trees as she was going through the woods. She could hardly pull it up the mountain with her, and she was all out of breath when she reached the top. She did not get to the bridge until it was dark. Then she was so afraid of dropping the basket into the river that she scarcely dared to step.

When at last she reached home she was tired out, but she pulled the screens close shut, so that no one could look in, and opened her treasure.

Treasure indeed! When she opened the basket she was horrified to find it full of spiders, slugs, worms, and bugs. To the sparrow this was a treasure of food, but to the woman it was disgusting.

When the mean, old woman saw the creatures in the basket she became so frightened that she jumped to her feet, ran screaming from her house, and was never seen or heard from again.

Lesson 9
Make Your Own Envelope

PURPOSE:
Resourcefulness is the key in this lesson, as your child learns to make his own envelopes.

MATERIALS NEEDED:
* Art Pattern #7 (page 73)
* Glue or paste
* Scissors

INSTRUCTIONS:
Using Art Pattern #7, have your child cut around the heavy lines. Fold the narrow sides on the dotted lines and apply glue on the top of those sides. Next, fold the wider part of the paper up, gluing it to the two sides. The envelope is now formed, with the flap ready to be folded down and glued, once a note is inserted. Using this pattern as a guide, your child can make many more envelopes by using various colors and types of paper.

FINAL THOUGHTS:
Since this is the section "Art for Others", we would suggest that you have your child send a note or picture to someone using their newly-made envelope. The art of letter writing is easily lost in an age of telephones, modems and faxes. Our own phone bill is proof of our need to improve in this area!

Your child does not have to write a letter if he is unable to do so. A picture he has drawn, or even an imaginative drawing sheet he has completed, would be a thoughtful way of sending his love to someone.

INTENSITY LEVEL: * (One Stars)

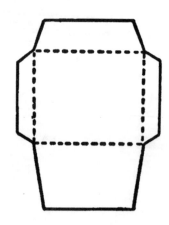 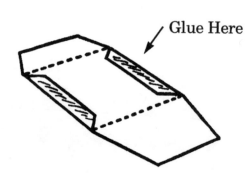 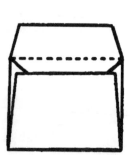

Glue Here

Lesson 10
Pomander Ball

PURPOSE:
In this lesson, your child will learn to create a scented object to enjoy for a long time to come or to give as a gift.

MATERIALS NEEDED:
* 1 medium orange
* 2 small jars of whole cloves
* Toothpicks (optional)
* Ground cinnamon for sprinkling on finished product

INSTRUCTIONS:
Press the cloves into the orange with the pointed ends down. If your child has difficulty inserting the cloves have him first puncture a small hole with a toothpick and then insert the clove. Keep the spacing of the cloves fairly close together. Realize that as the orange dries, it will shrink thus drawing the cloves closer. Once the orange is covered with the cloves, dust the entire ball with cinnamon and place it on a plate. Keep the pomander in a location with plenty of air circulation and turn it daily. Once it is fully dry, you have a fragrant and lasting decoration.

FINAL THOUGHTS:
It has been a Christmas tradition in our house to make one pomander ball each year at the beginning of December. Everyone takes a turn at the cloves and with five children to help, no fingers get too tired. We now have six pomander balls which we proudly display through the fall and winter in an antique wooden bowl, also occupied by pine cones. In the spring, we put it all in a tightly sealed plastic bag and store it away until the next fall.

While your pomander ball is in the drying stage, you can still display it attractively. We keep ours in the living room in order to enjoy the scent. One year we put it in an old carnival glass dish, another year it was in a willow ware bowl, and this year it was in pink depression glass. You can even hang the pomanders from a ribbon if you wish. However you choose to display the pomander is up to you and your child; just remember to have fun and be creative in the process.

INTENSITY LEVEL: * * (Two Stars)

Lesson 11
Wire Ornament

PURPOSE:
In this lesson, your child is provided with an idea for creating fun and easy ornaments for gift giving.

MATERIALS NEEDED:
* Thin craft or floral wire (12-18 inches in length)
* Newspaper to cover work surface
* White glue
* Two paper plates
* Glitter

INSTRUCTIONS:
Take the strip of wire, and have your child form it into a design. The wire can be shaped around a cookie cutter and then carefully removed, or he can create his own free-form shape. Be sure to leave enough excess wire at the top of the design to create a loop or hook for hanging.

Once the shape has been made, cover your working surface with newspaper and pour a shallow pool of glue on one paper plate and put the glitter on the other plate. Submerge all but the hook portion of the design into the glue and then into the glitter. Let the ornament dry thoroughly and touch-up spots which were missed with a little extra glue and glitter.

FINAL THOUGHTS:
Since these ornaments are flat and lightweight, they would be ideal for mailing. Your child may wish to make several to send to friends, so be sure to have extra supplies handy.

For future glitter work, not requiring the dipping involved in this project, save empty plastic spice jars. Pour in the glitter, snap on the lid and sprinkle away!

INTENSITY LEVEL: * * (Two Stars)

Lesson 12
Cornucopias to Give

PURPOSE:

In this lesson, your child will decorate and make a paper cornucopia which he can fill with tiny treats and give to a friend.

MATERIALS NEEDED:
* Sheet of white paper
* Glue
* Glitter, ribbon, stickers, etc. (optional)
* Colored pencils, crayons, or markers

INSTRUCTIONS:

Follow the instructions at the bottom of this page, and have your child shape the paper into a cone and then glue it closed along the edge. Using what materials you have available, have your child color and decorate the cone. If there is an upcoming holiday or celebration, you could suggest making that time a decorating focus. Once the decorating is complete, fill the cornucopia with small candies, wildflowers, or whatever you have available, and give it to someone who needs a "thank you" or a kind gesture.

FINAL THOUGHTS:

These cornucopias are reminiscent of May baskets which are hung on doorknobs the first day of May by anonymous well-wishers. If you wish to try this with the paper cornucopia, simply add a loop of ribbon to the top for hanging.

INTENSITY LEVEL: * * (Two Stars)

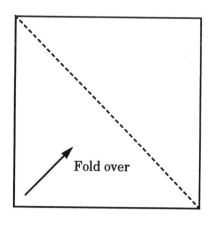

Fold over

Fold around and glue

Lesson 13
Silhouette

PURPOSE:
This lesson teaches your child how to make a silhouette, which he can give to a friend or family member.

MATERIALS NEEDED:
* Wall
* Chair
* Lamp with shade removed
* Pencil
* Two sheets of white drawing paper
* Tape
* Black construction paper

> *There's only one pretty child in the world, and every mother has it.*
>
> *--Chinese Proverb*

INSTRUCTIONS:
Move a chair sideways against a wall and seat your child in it so that his head is only a few inches from the wall. His head should be parallel with the plain of the wall. Next, place the lamp about ten feet from your subject, about the same height as your child's head, so that a strong shadow is thrown against the wall. Tape the paper to the wall, directly behind your child's head, and draw the outline of the shadow of your child's head on the paper. Take the drawing down from the wall and have your child cut it out. You should now have a white silhouette of your child's head.

The white silhouette can then be glued onto a piece of black paper, or you can reverse the process and draw the silhouette on black paper and glue it onto white. Either way, you end up with a nice side-view of your child's head. Instead of drawing the silhouette on black construction paper, you may also wish to color in the outline of the white silhouette with a black crayon or marker.

FINAL THOUGHTS:
If you want to share a few facts about silhouette art with your child, you can read these bits of information to him!

--Silhouettes were an eighteenth-century art form.
--Other names for this art were shadowgraphs, scissors art, shade art, skiagraphy and profile art.
--Silhouette art was an inexpensive and common substitute for painted portraits.
--Some silhouette artists prided themselves in being able to cut a profile freehand by sight alone.

INTENSITY LEVEL: * * * (Three Stars)

Lesson 14
Paper House

PURPOSE:

In this lesson, your child will cut out and glue together a pre-printed design to create a mini-house.

MATERIALS NEEDED:

* Art Pattern #8 (page 75)
* Scissors
* Glue or glue stick
* Crayons, markers, colored pencils or other coloring tools

INSTRUCTIONS:

Using Art Pattern #8, have your child color and decorate the house as he would like. Possible ways to design your miniature home may be by putting flower boxes under the windows for a spring or summer home, or by putting on wreaths and garland for winter. Once the coloring is complete, have your child cut out the house along the solid black lines. Fold along the dotted lines and glue the flaps down to the inside of the structure. Punch a hole in the circle at the top of the house, and your home is ready to hang.

FINAL THOUGHTS:

Feel free to photocopy extra "houses" for your child to use as gifts for others. Maybe a far away pen pal would enjoy a tiny gift like this. Simply leave it unglued and tuck it in with a note. Our 11 year old is always looking for things to send to his pen pal. This would be the kind of small item he would enjoy mailing!

INTENSITY LEVEL: * * * (Three Stars)

> Good art, like good science, describes the truth of a small or large part of reality without regard to maintaining the respectability of the artist. The fit subject for Christian art, therefore, is reality.
>
> --Franky Schaeffer, Sham Pearls for Real Swine

Lesson 15
All About YOU Collage

PURPOSE:
In this lesson, your child will create a collage of feelings and impressions about someone he cares for.

MATERIALS NEEDED:
*   Large piece of paper or poster board
*   Old magazines, photographs, words clipped from newspapers, etc.
*   Glue or glue stick

INSTRUCTIONS:
Cut out and glue onto the paper anything which reminds your child of the special person they have chosen. This can include words or phrases clipped from newspapers or magazines which praise him, or sound like something the person might say. Glue them in a collage format, overlapping as much as necessary. If your child takes the time to contemplate the interests and goals of the person chosen, the collage will be a treasured gift.

FINAL THOUGHTS:
This collage can be covered with clear contact paper for durability.

It is fun to see how children view the people around them. In making a collage like this, you may be amazed to see how observant of small details your child has been. Be careful not to discourage his choice of images, because his opinion will be unique from your own.

INTENSITY LEVEL: * * (Two Stars)

> Lives of great men all remind us
> We can make our lives sublime,
> And, departing, leave behind us
> Footprints on the sands of time.
>
> --Longfellow

Lesson 16
Crayon Muffins

PURPOSE:
Using scraps of crayons, your child can create a rainbow colored crayon muffin. These make great gifts to give to a friend.

MATERIALS NEEDED:
* Crayon pieces (paper removed)
* Paper cupcake liners
* Soup can
* Sauce pan
* Muffin tin

INSTRUCTIONS:
Remove all the paper from the crayons and sort them by color. Fill a saucepan with 1 to 2 inches of water and heat at medium temperature. Pinch one side of your clean soup can to make a pouring spout. Put one color of crayon in the can and heat in the water until the crayons are melted. <u>Warning</u>: Wax is very hot. An adult should do this part of the lesson due to the danger of burns!

Pour the melted wax into the cupcake liner and let cool. Continue adding colors until the crayons are gone or you have a thick muffin. You can hurry the cooling process along by putting the muffin tin in the freezer or outside on a cold day. Once the muffin is completely cool, peel off the paper and your child has a brand new rainbow crayon.

FINAL THOUGHTS:
You can wrap the crayon muffins in tissue paper for gift giving. This can make an inexpensive and thoughtful birthday or get-well gift. Just add a pad of paper and tuck them in a basket or small box. Your child's friend will be delighted. Don't forget to save one for yourself!

INTENSITY LEVEL: * * * (Three Stars)

Lesson 17
Yarn Bowl

PURPOSE:
In this lesson, your child will make a "catch-all" bowl using simple materials.

MATERIALS NEEDED:
* Various colors of yarn
* Paper bowl (heavy unwaxed type works best--Chinet brand; try to avoid styrofoam)
* Glue

INSTRUCTIONS:
Have your child swirl glue on the inside bottom of the bowl. Take the end of the yarn and begin wrapping it in a close fitting circular pattern. Continue going around the inside of the bowl, adding more glue as needed. Start a new piece of yarn whenever one runs out or you want to change colors. Continue in this pattern until the top edge of the bowl is reached. Wrap a piece of yarn around the edge and let it dry for a few minutes. Hint: This would be a good time to read a favorite story as you wait. After this break, flip the bowl over and proceed in the same fashion on the outside. Once completed, your bowl should be covered inside and out with yarn. Allow the bowl to dry thoroughly before filling with loose change, candy or other odds and ends.

FINAL THOUGHTS:
Extra yarn can be used to create yarn pictures. Trace a design on cardboard, run a bead of glue along the design and press the yarn into place.

If you want to learn more about the history of yarn design, you may want to research the yarn paintings of the Huichol Indians of northwest Mexico.

INTENSITY LEVEL: * * (Two Stars)

Section III Introduction

Children are very interested in making their own playthings. It isn't so much the making of the item as it is the messing around with all the raw materials. Observe children at play sometime and this will become readily apparent.

In our home, a skateboard and a sled are roped together to make a go-cart of sorts. Sticks become swords, guns, arrows, canes, etc. It is an unfettered childlike mind which is often the most inventive. Our desire is that your child will use the ideas here as a springboard toward inventions of his own.

"What makes people smart, curious, alert, observant, competent, confident, resourceful, persistent--in the broadest and best sense, intelligent--is not having access to more and more learning places, resources, and specialists, but being able in their lives to do a wide variety of interesting things that matter, things that challenge their ingenuity, skill, and judgment, and that make an obvious difference in their lives and the lives of people around them."
--John Holt *Teach Your Own*

Robinson Crusoe

Robinson Crusoe was a young English boy. He loved the water, and he loved the big ships. Every day he would dream about sailing away in a big ship with its white sails to find treasure and adventure.

Robinson's father was not happy about this. He wanted Robinson to stay home and get a good job. Many times he would talk with Robinson and tell him that it was not safe to be a sailor and that it would be better if he stayed home.

Robinson eventually left home and boarded a ship which was sailing across the ocean. This ship ran into a storm and was broken against some rocks. Of all the sailors on the ship, Robinson was the only one who lived through the storm.

Using a raft which he had made from broken pieces of the ship, Robinson moved as many supplies as he could from the ship to an nearby deserted island. He made many trips on his raft before the ship sunk into the water.

This story is about one of the adventures which Robinson had while living on his island.

Each day Robinson Crusoe labored long and patiently to make a shelter for himself, safe and comfortable. From some canvas he had found on the ship, he made a tent. Into this he put blankets for a bed, and boxes full of tools and food. Around the grassy spot that he had picked for his tent he built a high fence, with two rows of strong stakes driven deep into the ground. He made no door or gate to this fort, but climbed in and out by means of a high ladder that he pulled in after him each night.

So he lived, and a whole year went by. He had set up a large post on the spot where he had come ashore, and on this he cut a notch each day, to keep a record of time. He was fast learning how to protect himself, too, and how to make the things he needed.

One day, when he was out with his gun hunting food, he shot and wounded a mother goat. Rather than killing her, he decided to mend her wounds and try to raise her for a pet. This way he could start a little farm and have goat's milk and cheese whenever he wanted it. During the twenty-eight years he was on the island he was able to raise several goats and other kinds of animals.

In all that time he saw no other human being. Yet he wasted little energy in idle thoughts. The greatest comfort to him was his Bible. He set aside a little time each day for studying it, and always felt refreshed after this reading.

At first Robinson worried about food. What he had brought ashore from the ship would not last forever, and what would he eat when this was gone? But he caught plenty of fish and turtles and wild birds, and in time learned which of the birds and other wild animals were good to eat. "But how strange," he thought, "to be eating game and fish whose names I don't know! And how I would enjoy a slice of bread!"

Bread! Was there any way he could get bread? He had brought wheat grains from the ship. These he could plant, and when the wheat was ripe he could grind it into flour for bread.

But Robinson Crusoe knew nothing about farming, for he had grown up in a city. Spading the ground was easy, and he sowed his grains. But he planted at the wrong time of year, and none of the wheat came up. This was a bitter disappointment, but he had not used up all of his grains. He would try again. This time he fared better -- the little shoots came up, and presently he had fine stalks of wheat in his little plantation.

By the time his wheat was ripe, he had a plan for grinding it. He hollowed out a thick section of log, leaving the bottom in, so that he had something like a big bowl. Then he shaped a thick stick into a pestle, for pounding the wheat. So, grinding and pounding in this mortar, he made his flour. It took him a long time, and it was not very good flour, but it would make bread. Next time he would know how to go about the job better. Of course he saved some grains of this new wheat for next season's planting.

Then came the problem of finding something in which he could keep the flour. Many of his belongings he stored in baskets that he had taught himself to weave from grasses and reeds, but flour and certain other foods must be protected from dampness and from insects. Jars -- that was what he needed -- big earthenware jars with lids. But there had been none on the ship, and how was he to make any? He knew that clay was needed, and that after the jar had been molded into the right shape it must be dried in the sun.

He found some clayey earth, mixed it with water and shaped it as best he could in the form of a jar. This he set out in the sun to dry. But alas! It fell to pieces when he picked it up! He tried again and again, but was unable to make anything suitable in which to store his food. Then by accident, he found a large piece of clay which had broken off and fell into his fire. This piece of clay was very hard. He decided to try making some more pots, cups and dishes and baking them in the fire. His experiment worked. Now he could make all the bowls and dishes he needed.

It was the same with many other things he tried to do. At first he was awkward and things would turn out wrong. But he was learning patience, and he was building up confidence in his skills. Soon he began to feel that he could do anything that he needed to do.

Although Robinson Crusoe stayed on his island for many years before he was finally rescued, he learned a great deal about nature, himself, and God. Robinson's most important discovery was that God loved him, protected him from danger, and helped him to survive on the island.

Lesson 18
Tin Can Lanterns

<u>**PURPOSE**</u>:
In this lesson, we will design and make a lantern from an empty can.

<u>**MATERIALS NEEDED**</u>:
*   Can, washed and dried (soup or small coffee can)
*   Hammer or wood block
*   Large nail
*   Pliers
*   Paper to wrap can
*   Pencil, pen or marker
*   Water
*   Freezer
*   Bath Towel
*   Candle
*   Coat hanger, or other wire

<u>**INSTRUCTIONS**</u>:
Thoroughly wash the can and remove any wrappers. Fill the can with water and freeze until solid. Remove the can from the freezer and wrap with a piece of paper. On the paper, have your child design a pattern which he will later punch out with his hammer and nail. To make the holes, simply lay the can on a bath towel and gently hammer a nail into the can. The nail should go only 1/8 of an inch into the can. If the design is complicated, the can may have to be refrozen to solidify the ice again. Once the design is completed, punch one larger hole on each side of the can, near the top, for the handle. Run hot water over the can to remove the ice.

Using a piece of coat hanger or wire, insert each end into the handle hole and crimp the edge with your pliers to hold it securely. The handle should be long enough so your child does not burn his hand when he carries the lantern. Add the candle, and the lantern is complete!

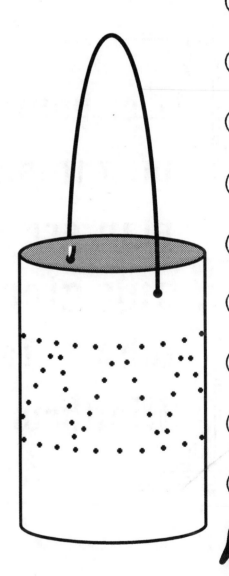

<u>**FINAL THOUGHTS**</u>:
These lanterns continue to be one of the most useful crafts our children have ever made. When the electricity goes out, they love to run and get their lanterns to add to the needed candle light. They also use the lanterns outside during evening picnics, which is great because the candle is slightly protected from the wind.

Do keep in mind that your child should not make the holes too close to the bottom of the can since melting wax may start trickling out.

<u>**INTENSITY LEVEL**</u>: * * * (Three Stars)

Let your light shine before men in such a way that they may see your good works, and glorify your Father who is in heaven. Matthew 5:16

Lesson 19
Fabric Banner

PURPOSE:
In this lesson, your child will learn how to construct a wall hanging made from readily available materials.

MATERIALS NEEDED:
*   Large scrap of fabric (old sheet or other colored fabric)
*   Two sticks (dowel rods, broom handle, twigs, etc.)
*   Glue
*   String
*   Fabric crayons, markers, paint, pieces of felt or fabric, etc.
*   Art Pattern #9 & #10 (page 77 & 79) (optional)

INSTRUCTIONS:
Have your child cut or trim the fabric to the desired shape. A good size would be 18 inches wide by 24 inches long. Turn the fabric over and place the stick at the top of the cloth and fold the fabric over the stick. Now you can choose to glue, staple or sew the edge in place. Repeat the same process at the bottom of the fabric. When this is complete, turn the banner right side up and your child may begin designing his banner. Designs could include a favorite verse, a slogan, a family crest, or simply drawings and designs. If using fabric crayons or markers, follow the package directions for heat setting the art work. If you are using felt or fabric to create a design, then you should lay all completed pieces out before beginning to glue them to the banner. Once the design is complete, attach a string to the top stick; and the banner is ready for display.

If your child is unable to think of anything to make, a sample banner design is available in Art Pattern #9 & #10. The pattern can be used as either a guide to color or to trace the fabric scraps. Your child can use all or any one of the graphics he chooses.

FINAL THOUGHTS:
If you really enjoyed working together on the banner, you may want to consider making one for each season of the year. Gather the family together and design a mutually agreed upon idea of what the upcoming season means to all of you. Serve a snack afterwards that goes along with the theme of the season you have been contemplating.

If your child collects various kinds of pins or buttons, he may enjoy using a blank banner to display his collection.

INTENSITY LEVEL: * * * * (Four Stars)

Lesson 20
Memory Holder

<u>**PURPOSE**</u>:

In this lesson, you will share with your child a way of compiling various forms of memorabilia into a special book.

<u>**MATERIALS NEEDED**</u>:

* Spiral notebook, photo album, ringed binder or other memory holder of your choice.
* Photos, news clippings, ticket stubs, ribbons, awards, brochures, or any other items which hold a special significance in the life of your child.
* Glue or tape
* Pen

<u>**INSTRUCTIONS**</u>:

Begin by talking with your child about his arrival into the family and all the special memories and events leading up to his present age. While you reminisce, you can begin gathering mementos to place in the book. You may create a simple book with a couple of pictures and a few sentences, or you may design a more elaborate keepsake album containing the items mentioned previously. However you choose to proceed is really irrelevant. The important goal is to create a sense of security and worth in your child. This will be his book to look through and save, knowing there can never be another one like it in the world!

This is a project which you will want to work on with your child for several years, or at least until he gets old enough to collect his own memorabilia.

<u>**FINAL THOUGHTS**</u>:

We took the memory holder idea a step further in our own family, by giving each child a memory box. This is simply a very sturdy cardboard box with a lid, (a plastic carton with a snap-on lid would also work). Into this box we placed assorted keepsakes. There are tollbooth tickets from trips, completed AWANA club workbooks, special letters, artwork, awards, pictures, etc.. This has worked well for our family because with five children, it is much easier to dump things into a box than to tape and glue them into a book. Besides, some bulky items would not fit well between the pages. We also have a spiral notebook in each box to record special memories and the changes in handwriting as each child gets older.

<u>**INTENSITY LEVEL**</u>: * * * * (Four Stars)

Lesson 21
Paper Buzzers

PURPOSE:
In this lesson, your child will learn how to make a fun and easy toy out of a strip of paper.

MATERIALS NEEDED:
*   Art Pattern #4 (page 65)
*   Scissors
*   A big breath of air
*   Extra paper

INSTRUCTIONS:
Cut out the long strip of thin paper in Art Pattern #4. Fold the paper in half lengthwise on the solid line and crease. Next fold each end of the strip on the dotted line and crease. Cut out the triangle in the middle of the folded end to form the mouthpiece. Your buzzer is now ready to go.

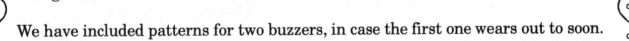

Holding the buzzer loosely between two fingers, have your child blow hard into the triangle to cause the paper to vibrate and buzz. Now that you have the hang of "buzzing", your child can experiment with new sounds. By cutting the paper in different size widths, and changing the size of the triangle mouth-piece, you are able to change the sound the buzzer makes.

We have included patterns for two buzzers, in case the first one wears out to soon.

FINAL THOUGHTS:
This is a craft which could be ideally used on those warm, sunny days, when your child is itching to get out of the house. He can take his buzzer outside and make lots of noise out of your earshot.

INTENSITY LEVEL: * (One Star)

Lesson 22
Imaginative Drawing "In the News"

PURPOSE:

As in an earlier lesson of this type, your child will be the "idea person" in a drawing project.

MATERIALS NEEDED:
* Art Pattern #11 (Page 81)
* Crayons, markers, colored pencils and other coloring tools

INSTRUCTIONS:

This imaginative drawing will put your child right in the headlines! Using Art Pattern #11, explain to your child that he must imagine a reason for being on the front page of a newspaper. Perhaps he became a daring hero, an olympic gold medal winner, or maybe he is just an all around great kid. Whatever he chooses is up to him; after all, everyone is entitled to their fifteen minutes of fame!

FINAL THOUGHTS:

If you have relatives who live in distant places, a fun and creative way of keeping in touch is by making a family newspaper. Different members of the family can write articles, draw pictures, or share a joke. The whole family can get involved this way, and the recipients feel involved and loved by your efforts.

Our two oldest boys sent a newspaper, they made for their grandparents, after a week-long visit in Minnesota. The boys enjoyed making the paper, and the grandparents especially enjoyed reading about the wonderful time everyone had. The grandparents even made copies and sent them to uncles and aunts the boys had also visited. Sending this newspaper was considered a very nice way to say thank-you for a great time.

INTENSITY LEVEL: * * (Two Stars)

The Brothers Gazette

Friday, October 1, 1993

Derek and Daniel Visit Minnesota

By Debbie Trulson
GAZETTE STAFF WRITER

CHICAGO – In a never before adventure, Derek and Daniel Trulson spent a whirlwind eight days in Minnesota. They enjoyed deluxe accommodations at the home of their grandparents in beautiful North Branch. They toured the State Park, searched for lost purses, befriended cats and dogs, created extra laundry and generally had a great time.

Derek and Daniel Trulson, Artwork by Daniel Trulson
10 and 9 play video games at Circus Pizza.

Another highlight was the time spent with Aunt Darla who enjoyed the opportunity to play at Pizza Circus and Camp Snoopy with the excuse that it was, "for the kids!" It must have been a great time for everyone because Derek and Daniel continued to remi-

Herbie dreams of good times and good food.

nisce about Aunt Darla and the time shared with her.

One low point occurred when the Minnesota Vikings beat the Chicago Bears during the brothers visit. Derek and Daniel remained loyal fans despite the presence of Viking supporters Deanna and Andy during the Sunday game.

Happily everyone overcame the rivalry to have a great time eating lasagna and laughing together. As Andy later said, "I think these kids have nearly turned me into a Bears fan!" Deanna was reported as saying, "I've always thought Chicago teams have cuter guys!"

The grand finale of the time consisted of a trip to Wisconsin and visits with Grandma Orne, Uncle Wilbur, Aunt Carole and Herbie. The brothers experienced farm life up close with pigs, horses, chickens and dogs. Despite the stimulating adult conversations, Derek and Daniel chose to spend the majority of their visit with Herbie, who was later overheard saying, "I'm glad they only come once a year so I have the time in between to rest up for the next visit." A baby pig was also quoted as saying, "I'll never get used to how boys smell!"

All in all the visit was a grand success and Great Grandma Orne thought so

too.

It was over too quickly in the eyes of Derek and Daniel, before they knew it they were on their way home. This time Grandma remembered her purse but she stated to a reported that she continues getting extra napkins at restaurants and periodically glances out the kitchen window to see if anyone has fallen out of a tree. Grandpa himself misses all the excitement and is keeping his chainsaw well oiled for the next visit.

As for Derek and Daniel, they were interviewed later upon their return to Chicago. Both brothers were full of stories and laughter but most of all they were thankful for the chance to be with all their relatives and have such a great time. They can't wait to return again but in the meantime they listen to their gift of Disney songs and remember the adventure.

*Final note: All quotes stated herein are written exactly as the reporter would like to have heard them.

Lesson 23
Fingerprinting

PURPOSE:
In this lesson, your child will use his fingerprint to make a variety of pictures.

MATERIALS NEEDED:
* Art Pattern #5 (Page 67)
* Finger
* Stamp pad, water colors or tempera paints
* Paper
* Pen, preferably felt-tipped marker

INSTRUCTIONS:
Have your child press his finger on the stamp pad, or brush his finger with paint and then press it on the paper. Using the examples in Art Pattern #5 and on this page, have your child create various items from his fingerprint. After the paint has dried, your child can draw the face and body features of whatever he created. Allow him the opportunity to be creative and develop his own designs. Fingerprinting is just as unique to an individual as a fingerprint!

FINAL THOUGHTS:
The fingerprint pictures on the Art Pattern and on this page were created by our children one afternoon as they eagerly poured over Ed Emberley's, *Great Thumbprint Drawing Book*. Look for it in your favorite bookstore or library.

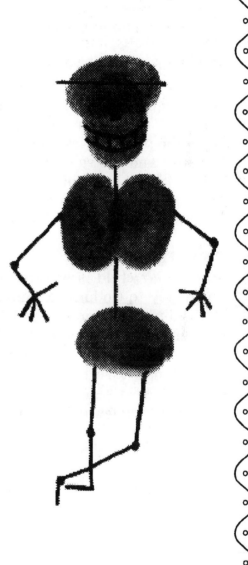

INTENSITY LEVEL: * * (Two Stars)

Lesson 24
Straw Painting

PURPOSE:
A straw will be the tool used in this lesson to create a unique painted effect.

MATERIALS NEEDED:
* Newspaper to cover work surface
* White paper
* Drinking straws
* Tempera paints, thinned with a small amount of water
* Containers for paint
* Teaspoon for each color of paint

INSTRUCTIONS:
Begin by covering your chosen work surface with a layer of newspaper. Separate your tempera colors into containers and add a few drops of water to thin the paints. You may have to experiment with the amount of water needed once you begin the project. Next, add spoons to each container, then give your child a sheet of paper and a straw. Have your child place a small spoonful of paint on his paper. Show him how to aim the straw at the paint and blow hard to create rivulets of paint across the paper. Continue using various colors until your child is satisfied with the achieved effect.

FINAL THOUGHTS:
When your child is working on projects involving paint or other substances unfriendly to clothing, a smock may be useful. Many different kinds of smocks are sold in craft stores or children's catalogs if you are interested in a ready made garment. Otherwise, one of dad's or mom's old shirts will work perfectly. We have found that t-shirts are preferable, since they can be easily slipped on and off with no buttons with which to contend. Don't worry about washing the smock each time it is used, since it will begin to take on a rather interesting abstract look of its own after a few paint splashes!

INTENSITY LEVEL: * * (Two Stars)

Lesson 25
Toothpick Sculpture

PURPOSE:
In this lesson, your child will sculpt a delicate design using only glue, toothpicks, and lots of imagination.

MATERIALS NEEDED:
* Flat toothpicks
* White glue
* Paper plate
* Small squares of wax paper

INSTRUCTIONS:
Pour a dollop of glue on the wax paper square. Give your child the paper plate and tell him that this will be the base of the sculpture. If your child is not familiar with sculptures, this may be a good time to visit one, or to look at pictures of them in a book. He must be able to visualize plans for his own towering edifice in order to begin building. The main idea in this project is to dip the toothpick ends into the glue and attach them together in order to create a climbing toothpick tower. Once it is completed to your child's satisfaction, allow the sculpture to dry, and then put it in a safe place for viewing.

FINAL THOUGHTS:
If you wish to make the structure more durable, you can coat it with spray shellac. You can also spray paint it another color for a different kind of look.

As we mentioned above, it is a good idea to investigate with your child various forms of sculpture. The goal of all these lessons is to act as an impetus toward further knowledge and experience. If you feel unable to teach or share a topic, don't worry about it. Children enjoy learning with adults and both groups benefit from the interaction.

If you want to make this a glue-free project, then simply take an idea from our five year old son. Just allow your child to lay the toothpicks in various designs on a flat surface, making as many designs as he wishes.

INTENSITY LEVEL: * * (Two Stars)

Lesson 26
Paddle Block Boat

PURPOSE:

In this lesson, your child will learn how to craft a boat, from a piece of scrap wood, to use for hours of fun.

MATERIALS NEEDED:
* Block of scrap wood (about 4 inches long, 2 inches wide, and 1 inch deep -- the rough end of a two-by-four works nicely)
* Thin piece of wood (about 1-2 inches long, 1 inch wide, and 1/4 inch deep)
* Two long nails
* Fat rubber band
* Hammer

INSTRUCTIONS:

Pound the two long nails into one end of the block of wood. Do not pound them all the way in, but just far enough to make them secure. Be sure to keep them as far apart as possible. Next, use a fat rubber band, about two inches long, (Hint: double it over the nails if you have to), and fit it over the nails. Slide the thin piece of wood between the rubber band, and wind up the paddle. Let go of the boat and watch it sail around in the bathtub or pond.

FINAL THOUGHTS:

Don't worry about the condition of the wood scraps. The point of this craft is to show how, by using just a few odds and ends around the house, one can make a fun toy. Keep in mind that this craft has been around for a long time. Our parents and grandparents would make toys like this to entertain themselves for hours. It is important to continue passing on these ideas so that, in an age of ready-made trinkets, children can still enjoy the simpler things of life.

INTENSITY LEVEL: * * * * (Four Stars)

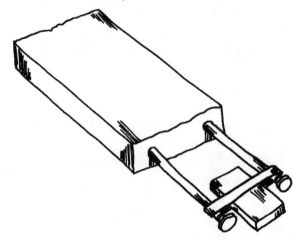

Lesson 27
Paper Beads

PURPOSE:
Many cultures make beads similar to the ones your child will make in this lesson.

MATERIALS NEEDED:
*   Bright colored magazines or catalog pages
*   Yarn for stringing beads
*   Metal washers or buttons
*   Watercolor paint brush handle or pencil
*   Glue or glue stick
*   Scissors

INSTRUCTIONS:
Cut the pages into 1 inch strips and lightly coat them with glue. Lay the center of the brush handle or pencil on one end of the strip. Fold that edge of the paper strip over the pencil and press it down. Place the palms of your hands on both ends of the pencil and gently wind towards the opposite end of the paper. Carefully remove the tool and lay the bead aside to dry. Once all the beads are completed, string them on the yarn. String the washers or buttons between the paper beads to create a more interesting piece of jewelry. Hint: Dip your yarn end into the glue and let dry, to make stringing the paper beads easier.

FINAL THOUGHTS:
The Egyptians made beads over 5,000 years ago. In fact millions of beads were woven into the coverings for mummies!

INTENSITY LEVEL: * * (Two Stars)

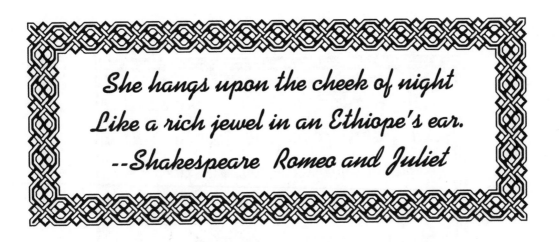

She hangs upon the cheek of night
Like a rich jewel in an Ethiope's ear.
--Shakespeare Romeo and Juliet

Lesson 28
Finger Glove Puppets

PURPOSE:
Recycling old rubber gloves into a fun plaything is the goal of this lesson.

MATERIALS NEEDED:
* Rubber kitchen glove(s)
* Scissors
* Glue
* Permanent markers
* Yarn scraps, wiggly eyes, beads, fabric or felt bits, etc.

INSTRUCTIONS:
Cut off as many fingers as can be salvaged from an old pair of rubber gloves. Have your child decorate and design the rubber fingers in whatever way he wants. Yarn scraps make great hair, and felt bits can become clothes or facial features. Just lay all the supplies out and see what becomes of it. Remember, look around for bits and pieces of materials instead of purchasing unnecessary items. Once the creating is done, a puppet show would be a great finale!

FINAL THOUGHTS:
Two-sided puppets can be made by simply designing a different face for each side of a glove finger. For example, one side could be happy and the other side sad.

INTENSITY LEVEL: * * (Two Stars)

...The education of even a very small child, therefore, does not aim at preparing him for school but for life.
--Maria Montessori

Section IV Introduction

In the following nature crafts, we will show your child how to create things from what is readily available around you. As often as possible, we attempt to keep away from useless craft items. Instead, we hope to spur both you and your child toward a greater appreciation of all that surrounds us.

Many times people try to excuse their lack of interest in beauty by saying they are not "talented" or "artistic". The truth may more often be in a lack of training the mind's eye to recognize beauty. We must work at heightening our senses to distinguish between the ordinary and the extraordinary.

Look around you; have you made your child's environment a sensory experience? This is vital to their outlook on art. The first memories of creativity are built directly into their environment. Do they see objects displayed upon which their eye can linger? Do they smell food that has taken love and time to prepare? Are there books for the imagination and music for the ear? Begin taking the time to make you and your child aware of the many facets of art. Hopefully, you will start that journey with your child in a small way as we sample bits and pieces of the natural world around us.

"The Christian is the one whose imagination should fly beyond the stars."
--Francis A. Schaeffer *Art and the Bible*

The Caterpillar Story

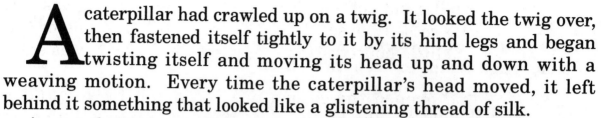

A caterpillar had crawled up on a twig. It looked the twig over, then fastened itself tightly to it by its hind legs and began twisting itself and moving its head up and down with a weaving motion. Every time the caterpillar's head moved, it left behind it something that looked like a glistening thread of silk.

An ant that was crawling along the branch stopped and stared with wonder. "What in the world are you doing?" it asked.

The caterpillar paused to rest for a moment. It was hard work, bending and doubling itself in that way. "I'm making a house," it said.

"Making a house!" cried the ant.

A bee that had lighted close by began to buzz with laughter. "Will you tell me, if you please, what sort of house that is?" he cried.

"The only sort of house I know how to make," the caterpillar answered humbly.

"I never heard of anything so absurd. Why don't you hunt about and find a hollow tree, or a good hive, and live in that? Then you would be safe."

"Or you might find a hole under a stone," added the ant. "That's a very good place."

The caterpillar shook its head. "This is the only sort of house I know how to make," it repeated. Then it set to work again.

As for the bee and the ant, they went their ways.

"A poor sort of a house indeed," each one thought to itself.

But the caterpillar went on working.

Up and down, up and down its head moved, weaving and weaving. Now the silk was like a thin, silvery veil about it. Through the veil, you could still faintly see the caterpillar moving.

At last the veil grew so thick that you could not see the caterpillar at all. You could only guess that it might still be at work inside.

After a while, the bee came by that way again.

It stopped and looked the little house all over. Then it flew down to the ant-hill. "Miss Ant, Miss Ant, come out here," it buzzed. "I've such a joke to tell you."

The little ant stuck its head up from the hill.

"Such a joke! That caterpillar we were watching has finished its house, and has forgotten to leave any door," and the bee buzzed very hard.

"That is too bad," said the ant, "I'm afraid it will starve."

But the caterpillar did not die. It was not even hungry. It was fast asleep in its little cocoon house. While it slept, the sun shone or the rain beat, but the little house let in neither sun nor rain. It was snug and dark.

If anyone had opened the cocoon now, he would have found a wonderful thing. Inside the hard, gray outside shell was a lining as soft as silk, and still inside of this was something -- what was it? Not a caterpillar, not a butterfly either, though if one looked carefully one could see what looked like tiny wings folded closely down each side of folded legs, and the shape of feathery antennae such as butterflys have, but these, too, folded closely down. All were sealed together in what looked like a brown, soft skin. This thing was what we call a pupa.

Days and nights passed and at last what had once been the caterpillar began to stir and wake.

"How strange I feel! How strange I feel!" said the thing to itself. "I must have light and air."

One end of the cocoon was very soft and loose. It was through this end that what had once been the caterpillar pushed its way out into the air.

Oh, how weak it felt! Fastened to it on each side were two crumpled wet things, which it began to move feebly up and down. As it moved them, it felt its strength returning; and the crumpled things began to spread and dry. Broader and broader they spread until they were strong, velvety wings, two on each side. They were of the most beautiful soft brown color, with a pinkish border along the edges. In the middle of each of the lower wings was a glistening spot like the "eye" spot on a peacock's feather.

This thing was no longer a caterpillar; it had become a beautiful winged butterfly.

Presently it walked from the twig down upon the gray cocoon, within which it had lain so long. Then it spread its wings and floated softly off through the air and down to the earth. It did not fly far, for it had not its full strength as yet.

When it alighted, where should it be but on the ant-hill! The little ant was very busy there, tugging at twigs and leaves, and hunting for food. It stopped its work to stare with awe at the wonderful stranger. "You beautiful thing," it said "where did you come from?"

"Don't you remember the caterpillar that made itself a house on the twig above?"

"Oh yes, poor thing, it must have died long ago," said the ant. "I went up there once or twice to see if I could help it, but there was no sound or stir."

"I am that caterpillar," said the butterfly gently.

The ant stared and wondered. "I was once a pupa myself," it cried. "But I did not hatch out with such wings as those."

Just then who should come buzzing by but the very bee that had laughed at the caterpillar's house. It, too, stopped to gaze at the wonderful stranger. When it learned that this butterfly was that very caterpillar, it buzzed for wonder. "Well, well!" it said, "so that was what you were about, was it; growing wings in your weird house!"

But the caterpillar stirred itself. "Now I must go," it said. "I must find a shelter under a rock or in some hollow tree until the sun goes down. But tonight -- ah, tonight! Then I shall come out to fly wheresoever I will."

So it waved its great wings and flew softly and noiselessly away out of sight.

The ant and the bee sat looking after it. "And to think," cried the bee, "that we did not understand what that caterpillar was doing! It appears, after all, that each creature knows his own business best."

Lesson 29
Milk Carton Bird Feeder

PURPOSE:
In this lesson, your child will make a feeder for our feathered friends.

MATERIALS NEEDED:
*   Cardboard milk carton
*   Sharp knife or scissors
*   Twig or dowel rod (long enough to go through the carton, leaving a perch on either side
*   Bird seed or sunflower seeds
*   String

INSTRUCTIONS:
Cut two square openings on either side of the milk carton leaving about one inch of frame around the outside. This is the only part of the craft which you should either do yourself or closely supervise. Make a hole beneath the openings on each side and insert the twig or dowel to create perches. Make a small hole in the top of the carton and thread a string through to hang from a tree branch. Fill your feeder with bird seed and hang it outside for the birds to enjoy. Although, if your yard is anything like ours, you may be fattening up all the squirrels as well! Attempt to hang your feeder where it is easily visible from a window; this way your family can watch the birds from the house.

FINAL THOUGHTS:
You may also create a bird feeder from a plastic milk jug using the same design as the cardboard carton.

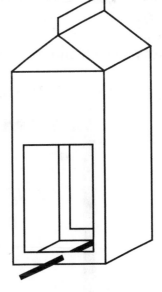

Another idea to consider, if you have more than one child doing this project, is using pint cartons. Each child could create a mini-feeder of their own and then be in charge of refilling the seed when it is eaten. Remember that once you begin feeding birds, especially in the fall, you must continue doing so; as they will stay nearby and rely upon your provision. In addition, it may take a week or more for the birds to find your feeder, so make sure your child does not expect instant results.

INTENSITY LEVEL: * * (Two Stars)

Lesson 30
Stone Painting

PURPOSE:
In the following project, your child will hunt for a rock in which he sees a naturally formed design.

MATERIALS NEEDED:
* Powers of observation
* Crawling around outdoors clothes
* Markers or paints

INSTRUCTIONS:
Choose a day for this endeavor when the weather is conducive to digging around under bushes and sifting through dirt. Before beginning the hunt, explain to your child that he should find a rock or rocks which look like something other than what they are. For example, maybe he will see an animal shape, or a face, or whatever his mind imagines. When your child finds his "treasure," the rock should be washed and allowed to dry. At this time, your child can use the markers or paint to enhance the image he sees.

FINAL THOUGHTS:
This can be the start of a fun collection, although you may want to limit the size of rocks allowed; after all, a house can only hold so many boulders! It is amazing though, what children can see that sometimes passes by our impatient adult eyes. Our seven year old found rocks which he designed to look like a beagle, a ladybug and a robin's egg. Another son, knowing how we collect everything heart-shaped, was overjoyed one summer to find a perfectly heart-shaped rock. It now merits a coveted place on our bucket bench. Once again, it is fascinating to contemplate the beauty to be found in the most ordinary of objects.

INTENSITY LEVEL: * * (Two Stars)

The stone which the builders refused is become the head stone of the corner.

Psalm 118:22

Lesson 31
Tin Foil Dinners

PURPOSE:
In this lesson, we will provide for you and your child a recipe for outdoor dining.

MATERIALS NEEDED:
* Heavy duty tin foil
* Ground meat formed into patties about 3/4 to 1 inch thick (amounts depend upon the number of people being served -- you be the judge)
* All purpose potatoes sliced 1/8 inch thick
* Carrots sliced
* Onions sliced
* Green pepper sliced (optional)
* Butter
* Salt
* Pepper
* Charcoal, grill, cooking supplies

INSTRUCTIONS:
Tear off a 12-18 inch sheet of heavy duty tin foil for each dinner being prepared. Place about 1/2 tablespoon of butter in the center of each piece of foil. Put the hamburger patty on top of the butter. Pile potato and carrot slices on the meat (amount depends upon each person's appetite). Top with a couple slices of green pepper and onion, and then sprinkle with salt and pepper. Next, you must fold all the sides of the foil tightly together to form a pouch. There must be no open edges through which the juices can escape. The best way to create the pouch is to bring up the four corners of the sheet to a point, then crimp together the edges of the foil. Your pouch should look like a pyramid when you are finished.

Place the dinners on your hot grill and cook until the meat and potatoes are done. Depending upon the temperature of your coals, this could take 10 to 20 minutes. If at all possible, enjoy your meal outdoors. Everything seems to taste better when it is eaten under a canopy of sky.

FINAL THOUGHTS:
These tin foil dinners are meant to be shared as a family celebration. There is virtually no cleanup as the meal is already self-contained. We especially enjoy eating by the light of 4 or 5 of our kerosene lanterns. After the meal is completed, we each take a lantern and go for a late night walk around our neighborhood. The previously described tin-can lanterns (Lesson #18) would be fun to light and use during your outdoor meal.

It is important to remember that not every activity which we present to you can be done completely by your child without any help from you. Perhaps your child could slice potatoes and carrots, or maybe he could form the hamburger patties. Do not be concerned about doing parts of a project yourself, unless of course, you are simply interfering in order to make it "your way". The closeness imparted through working and creating together is the artistic beauty we hope to foster.

INTENSITY LEVEL: * * (Two Stars)

If we want interesting, obedient children, we as parents have to be interesting ourselves and obedient to Christ. We have to read, watch, and listen. If we want children who are interested in culture, then our children must see our interest. If we want the truth about Jesus Christ to be interesting to our child, then, our own lives, which we claim are based on the truth, must compete with the interest, diversity, beauty, artistic creativity, and intelligence often found in the non-Christian community.
--Franky Schaeffer *Sham Pearls for Real Swine*

Lesson 32
Seed Wreath

PURPOSE:
In this lesson, your child will use various seeds and beans to create a natural looking wreath.

MATERIALS NEEDED:
*   Art Pattern #12 (Page 83)
*   An assortment of dried beans and seeds
*   A strong piece of cardboard (pizza box cardboard works great!)
*   Glue
*   Scissors

INSTRUCTIONS:
Explore with your child all the ways of obtaining seeds for this project. Perhaps there are pods and seeds outside your house which you could gather. Also, wash and dry seeds from fruits and vegetables which your family eats, (watermelon, oranges, lemons, pumpkins, squash, etc.). You can also use some dried peas and beans from the grocery store. The most fascinating wreath mosaics usually contain a variety of seeds and beans from all these sources.

Once you have a good assortment of seeds, you are ready to begin the project. Using Art Pattern #12, trace the design onto your cardboard. Cut the cardboard according to the pattern, forming a donut-shaped wreath. You may at this point, want to allow your child some quiet time to sort through his seeds and plan a pattern for the wreath. Once he is ready to begin, have him apply glue to small areas, and then, position the seeds and beans to create his pattern. Continue around the circle in this manner until it is complete. Allow the wreath to dry completely before hanging.

FINAL THOUGHTS:
You could try many different cardboard shapes for this project. These could also make a special kind of gift uniquely created by your child. If your child finds the work too tedious to complete, try saving it for the next day, or maybe working on it together.

INTENSITY LEVEL: * * * * (Four Stars)

Lesson 33
Ivy Sculpture

PURPOSE:
This lesson allows your child to observe the growth of plant life as he trains ivy vines to grow into a simple shape.

MATERIALS NEEDED:
*   Newspapers to cover work surface
*   Flower pot (about 6 inches high, 6-8 inches wide)
*   Potting soil
*   Dry sheet (optional)
*   2 or 3 small ivy plants (starts)
*   Wire coat hanger
*   Two pliers

INSTRUCTIONS:
Lay newspapers down to catch any dirt spills. Have your child fill their flower pot about 3/4 full of soil. Next, have them carefully put their plants in the dirt, covering them with more potting soil to reach one inch from the top of the pot. Do not place the ivy directly in the middle of the container, because the vining wire will go there.

To make the vining wire, untwist your coat hanger so you have a straight wire to begin shaping. Your child may need help in this area. The simplest design is a circle, but you can form a heart or other shape if you are interested. As you bend your wire, make certain to leave 2-3 inches at each end. These ends are twisted together and stuck into the middle of the pot. Press the wire into the soil until it stands firmly, being careful not to injure your ivy plant.

If your ivy is large enough, you can begin training it around the wire; otherwise, it will take several weeks for the ivy to grow so it can be sculpted to the design. Show your child how the vine will wrap around the shape with their help in training it. Remind him that the growth process takes a while, but eventually, they will have their very own plant sculpture. This is a good object lesson for your child. Each of us are like the ivy plant; it takes a wise parent to train and guide us.

FINAL THOUGHTS:
To give your plant a dressier look, you can buy sheet moss to place on the top of the soil. The ivy can be planted in any kind of pot available, so don't worry about running out to buy anything.

INTENSITY LEVEL: * * * (Three Stars)

Lesson 34
Colored Sand Picture

PURPOSE:

In this lesson, your child will create a picture using sand which he has tinted various colors.

MATERIALS NEEDED:
* Fine, clean sand
* Glue in squeeze bottle
* Food colors or tempera paints
* Small containers for batches of sand
* White poster board (shirt cardboard, gift box top, or purchased poster board cut to size)
* Pencil
* Tiny shells or pebbles (optional)

INSTRUCTIONS:

To tint the sand, separate it into the containers (baby food jars or clean yogurt cups work well). Add a few drops of food coloring or tempera paint, and mix.

To make the picture, your child may wish to lightly sketch a design with his pencil; or he can design his picture free form. Next, have your child cover his design with glue and sprinkle the color of sand he prefers, on each part. Hint: you may want to let the glue dry for a few minutes between each color you sprinkle. After the sprinkling is complete, let the picture dry completely and shake off the excess sand.

If your child would like to frame his work, he can glue small shells or pebbles around the edges of his picture. You may need a heavier "craft type" glue to hold the shells or pebbles securely.

FINAL THOUGHTS:

If you decide to hang this sand masterpiece, you can glue a heavier piece of cardboard to the back of the poster board. This will keep the picture from curling at the edges.

Sand art has become popular at fairs and craft shows. You can actually pay several dollars to layer colored sand in a bottle similar to our previous "Beans in a Bottle" project. This might be a fun use for any leftover colored sand you have after this lesson.

INTENSITY LEVEL: * * * (Three Stars)

Lesson 35
Imaginative Drawing

PURPOSE:
In this lesson, your child will be the "idea person" as he completes this drawing project.

MATERIALS NEEDED:
* Art Pattern #13 (Page 85)
* Crayons, markers, colored pencils or other coloring tools

INSTRUCTIONS:
Using Art Pattern #13, your child will need to imagine a suitable picture to draw inside the door. You may use the storyline below to help you be creative.

You have been given the special task of drawing a picture to hang in the window of an art gallery. Using your imagination, draw a picture of whatever you think will please God. What picture does your mind's eye bring before you?

FINAL THOUGHTS:
Young children will often need help in the development of their God-given creativity. It is important, therefore, for teachers to provide young students with projects that can help them draw, paint, or color images that are special to them. The expressions of each individual are important. God can use the unique thoughts of children and adults to bring forth powerful images that can minister to people. Children need to see that art is sometimes a dream that is yet to be painted.

INTENSITY LEVEL: * (One Star)

She was inside the wonderful garden and she could come through the door under the ivy any time and she felt as if she had found a world all her own.
--Frances Hodgson Burnett, *The Secret Garden*

Lesson 36
Eggheads

PURPOSE:
In this lesson, your child will discover a new way to watch seeds sprout and grow.

MATERIALS NEEDED:
* Eggshells
* Egg carton
* Soil
* Grass seeds
* Permanent marker

INSTRUCTIONS:
Save your eggshells in advance of this project. The best shells are the ones which are broken evenly across, and make up 3/4 of the egg. After collecting the shells you want to use, have your child draw a funny face on the shell. Examples are shown on the right. (Hint: Try to draw the eyes high enough to make them peer above the carton.)

Now fill the shells with soil, sprinkle grass seed on them, and moisten them with water. Place the carton in a sunny window and soon your eggheads will have funny hair. Style them with scissors when needed and watch their hair "grow" again.

FINAL THOUGHTS:
When your child is finished enjoying his slightly cracked friends, plant them outside. The shells, as they decay, provide minerals for the earth.

ANGRY ASTONISHED

SURPRISED HAPPY

MEAN BEWILDERED

SLY GOOFY

Children are fascinated with observing the sprouting of seeds. One way our children view this is by cultivating our own alfalfa sprouts. It only takes a couple of days before the sprouts show and then a couple more days to be ready to eat. They are delicious, nutritious and easy to grow.

INTENSITY LEVEL: * * * (Three Stars)

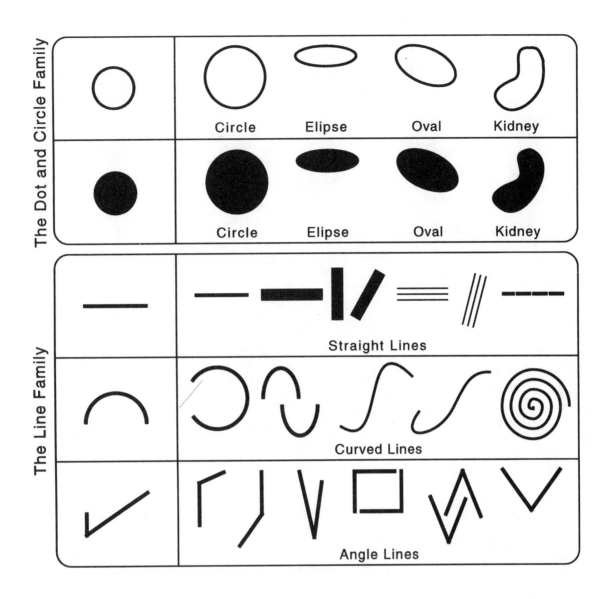

The Dot and Circle Family

Circle Elipse Oval Kidney

Circle Elipse Oval Kidney

The Line Family

Straight Lines

Curved Lines

Angle Lines

*Idea for the five elements of shape borrowed from
<u>Drawing With Children</u> by Mona Brookes

The Dot and Circle Family

Circle   Elipse   Oval   Kidney

Circle   Elipse   Oval   Kidney

The Line Family

Straight Lines

Curved Lines

Angle Lines

*Idea for the five elements of shape borrowed from
Drawing With Children by Mona Brookes

Art Pattern #3, to be used with Lesson #6, page 11.

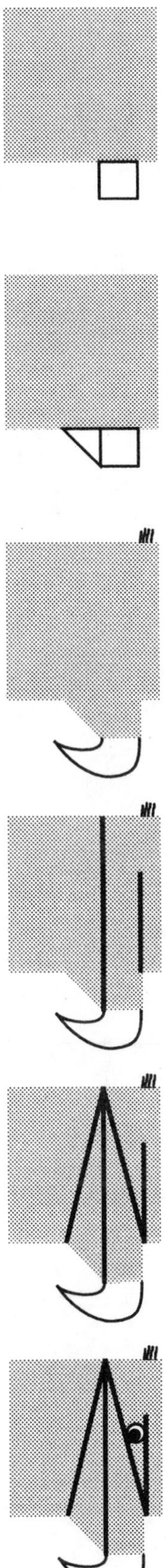

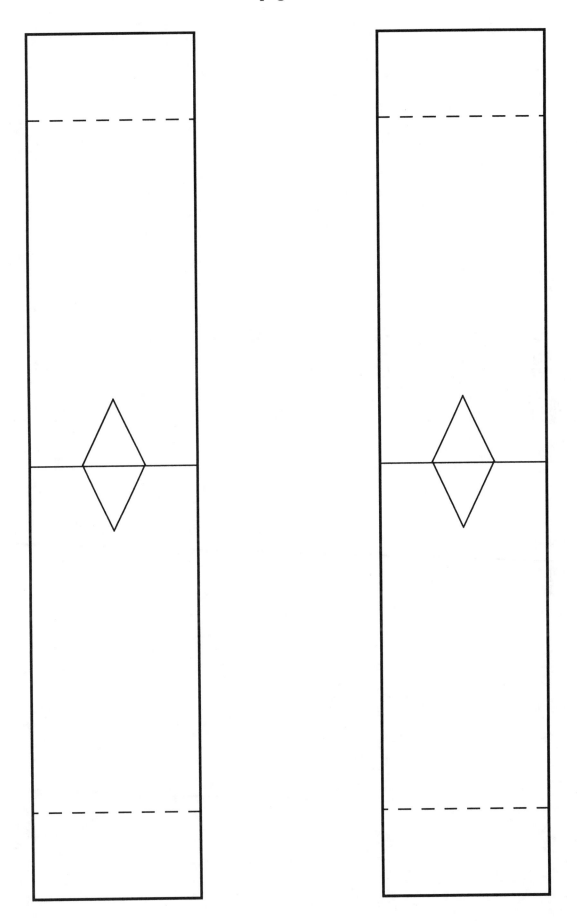

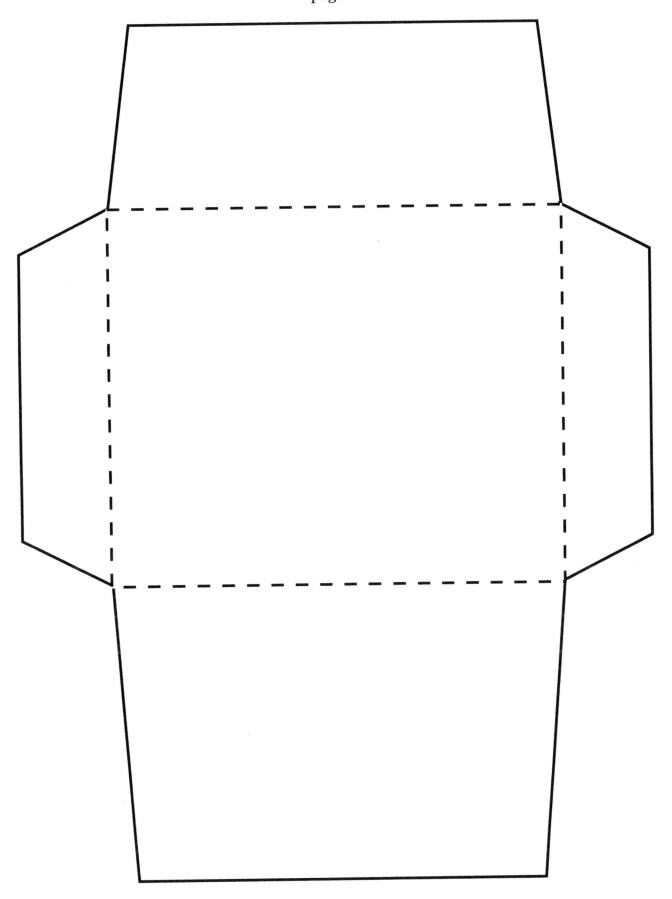

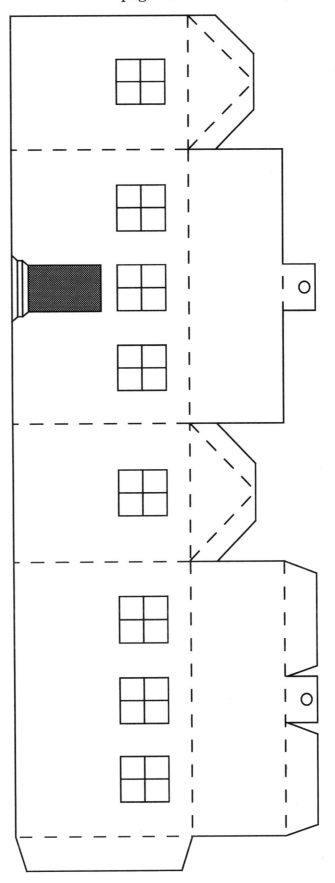

JESUS

LOVES

ME

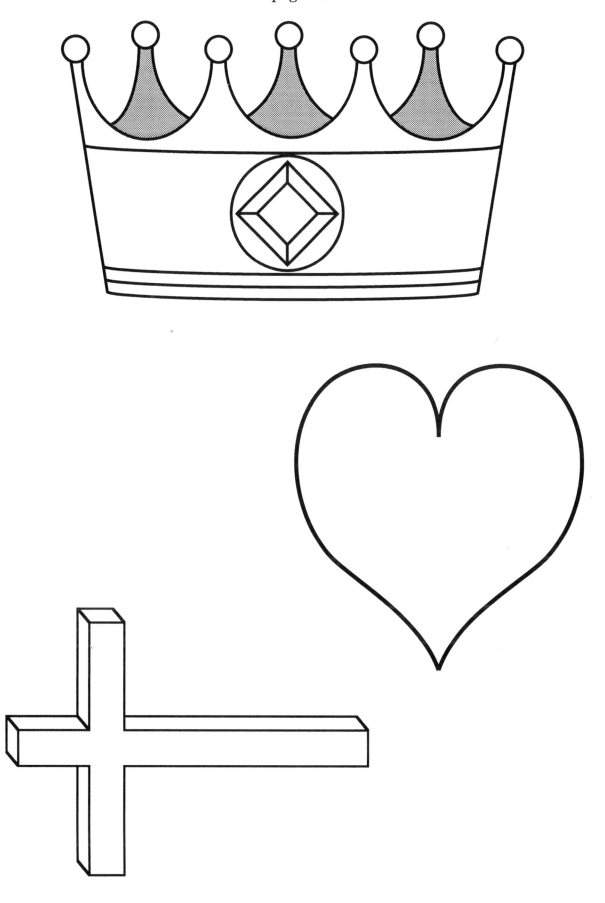

The Daily Times

Local Youth Makes it Big!

Picture here of local youth, doing what comes naturally!

Art Pattern #12, to be used with Lesson #32, page 51.

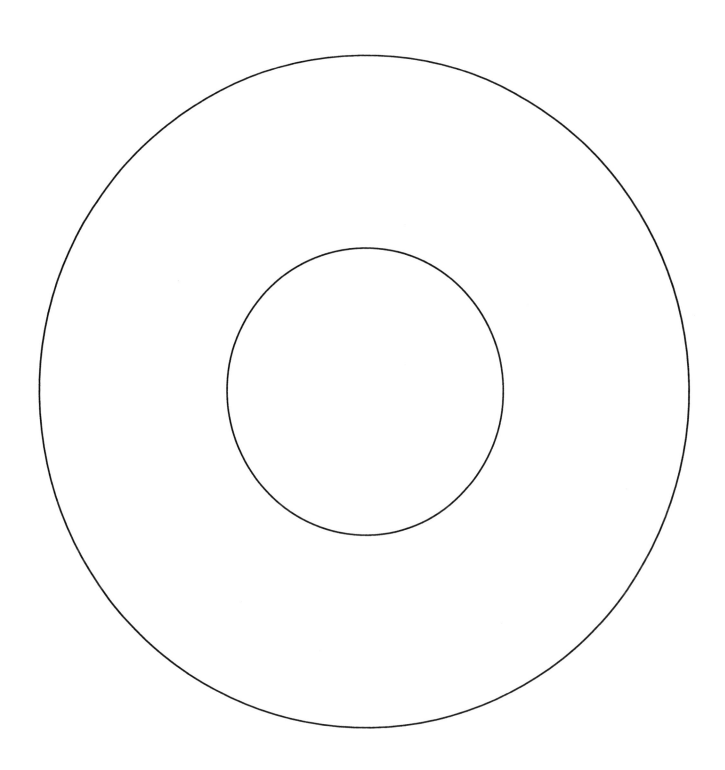

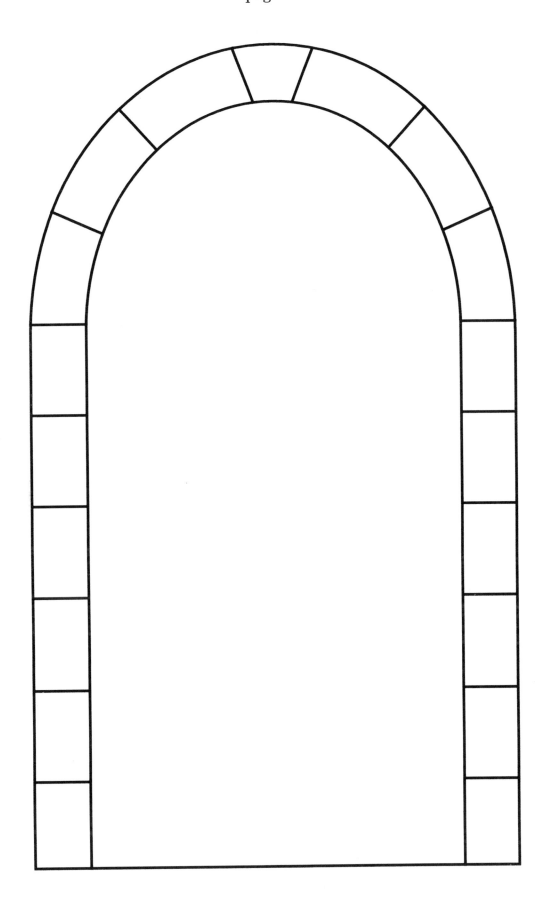